The Happy Book

50 RAYS OF SUNSHINE TO BRIGHTEN YOUR DAY

ANDREA REISER

PickleStar Press
New York

Published by PickleStar Press

ISBN 978-0-692-10741-6

Printed in the United States of America

10 9 8 7 6 5 4 3 2 1

Start each day with a
grateful heart

You are capable of AMAZING things

Positive Mind.
Positive vibes.
Positive Life.

Life
begins
at the end of your
comfort
zone

Be fearless in pursuing what sets your soul on fire

Know that your kindness
has a ripple effect
in the universe

she
designed
a life
she loved

Dream BIG

Aim HIGH

Reach BEYOND THE STARS

And don't EVER stop believin'

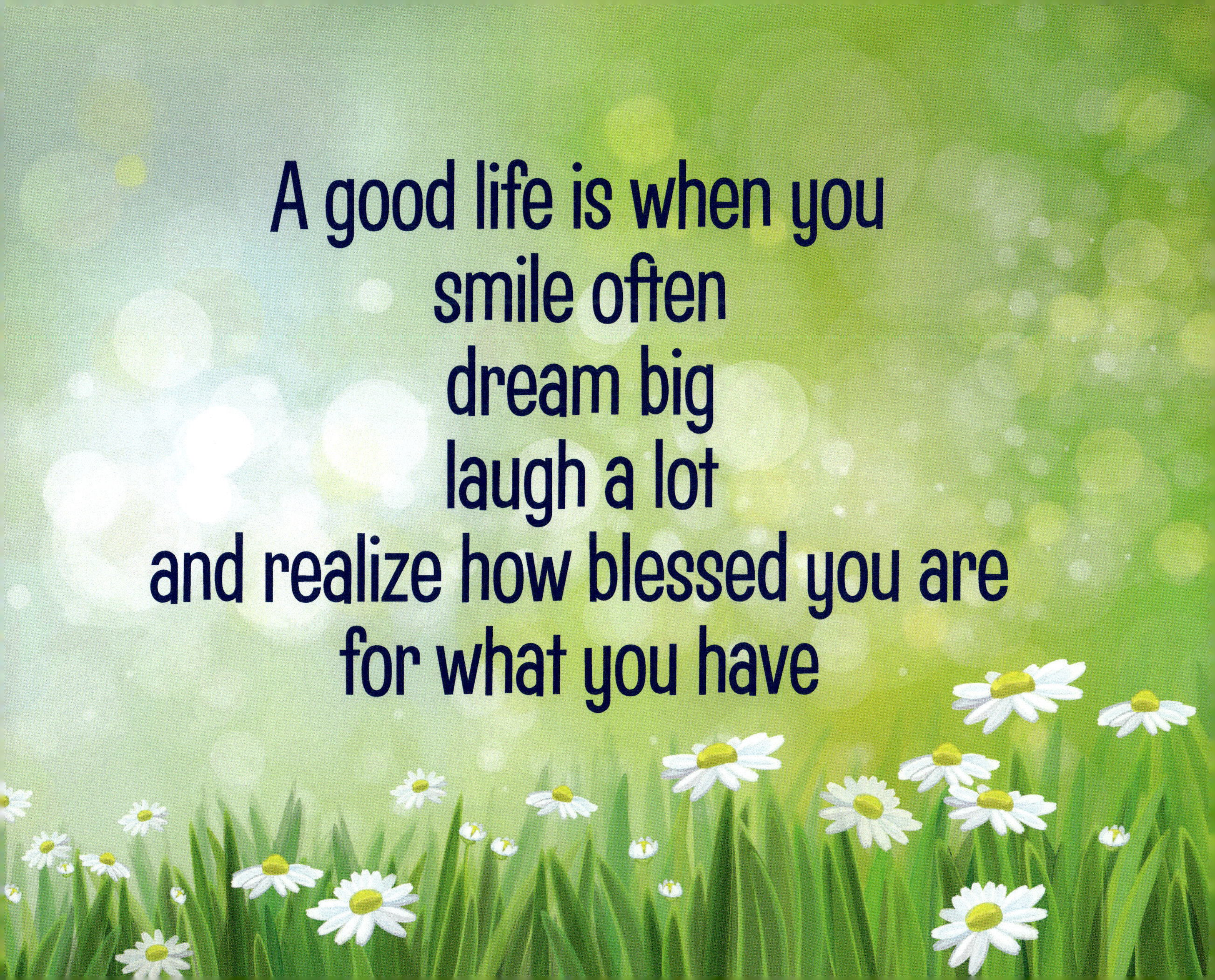
A good life is when you
smile often
dream big
laugh a lot
and realize how blessed you are
for what you have

BE SOMEONE'S
SUNSHINE
WHEN THEIR SKIES
ARE GRAY

THE SECRET
TO HAVING IT ALL
IS BELIEVING YOU DO

IT'S THE
LITTLE THINGS
IN LIFE

THERE IS
always
always
something to be
THANKFUL FOR

Whatever you do today, do it with love

Be your own kind of Beautiful

To the world
you may be one person,
but to one person
you may be the world

Look at all you've survived in the past.
You'll get through this, too.

Collect moments,
not things

Actually,

I can

and

I will

YOU ARE
DAZZLING
WISE
EMPOWERED
AND COURAGEOUS

Do something
that makes
your ♥ sing
every single day

she took a
deep breath
& let it go

EVERY ENDING IS A NEW BEGINNING

The sky is the limit

Everything we see depends on how we look at it

Live with no regrets

Alive.
Blessed.
Grateful.

LIFE IS BETTER WHEN YOU'RE LAUGHING

Don't let anyone dull your sparkle

Today's little moments become tomorrow's precious memories

GOOD FRIENDS ARE LIKE STARS...

YOU DON'T ALWAYS SEE THEM,
BUT YOU KNOW THEY'RE ALWAYS THERE.

When it rains,
look for rainbows.
When it's dark,
look for stars.

Find joy
in the
simple things

BELIEVE IN YOURSELF
AND YOU WILL BE
UNSTOPPABLE

If you can lie down at night
knowing in your heart
that you made someone's day
just a little bit better,
you know you had a good day

You are

STRONGER

than you feel

Make delicious things
with life's lemons

Every day may not be good,
but there's something good in every day

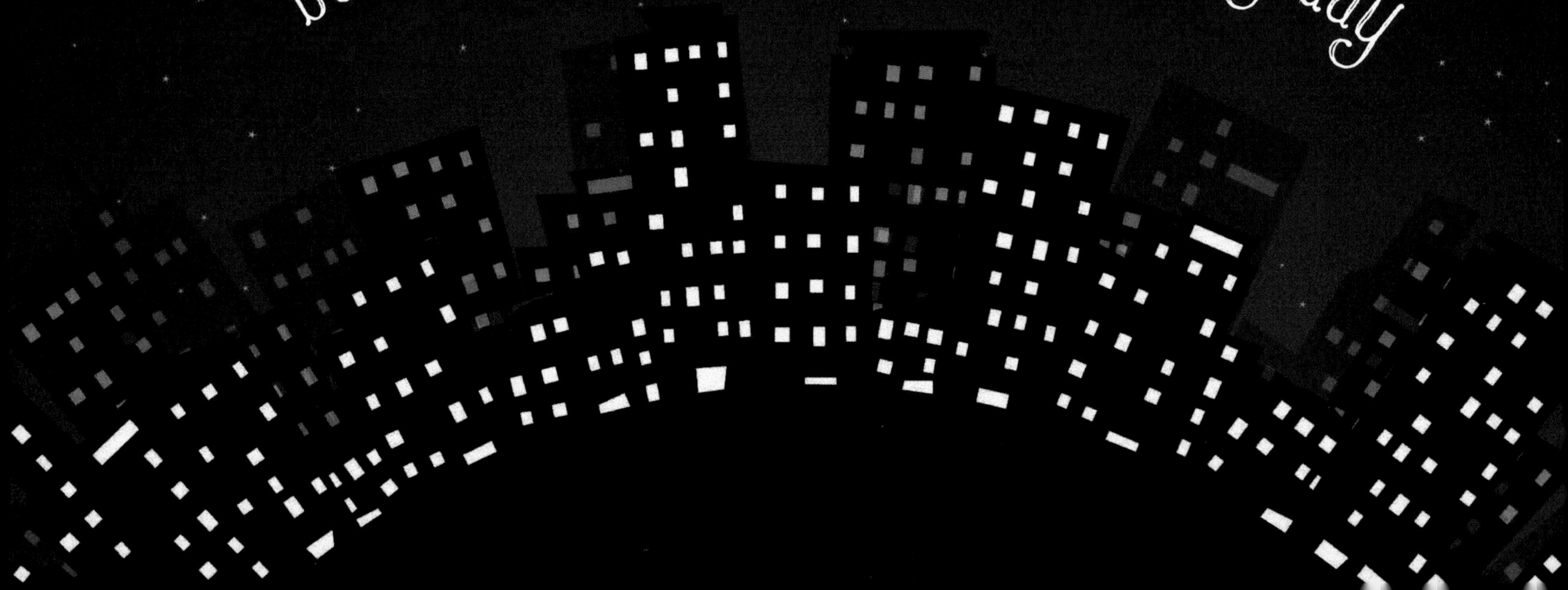

CONFIDENCE

IS BEAUTIFUL AND POWERFUL

When you love what you have,
you have everything you need

Wherever you are, be all there

MAKE TODAY
SO AWESOME
YESTERDAY
GETS JEALOUS

Difficult roads
often lead
to beautiful destinations

Take a moment
to remind someone
how amazing they are

Some days you just have to create
your own sunshine

IT'S A WONDERFUL DAY
FOR A WONDERFUL DAY!

Surround yourself
with people
who see your value
and remind you of it

If
you're
searching
for that one person
who will change your life...

TAKE A LOOK IN THE MIRROR

I don't know what lies ahead,
but I sure am grateful
for the journey so far

AND DON'T YOU FORGET IT!

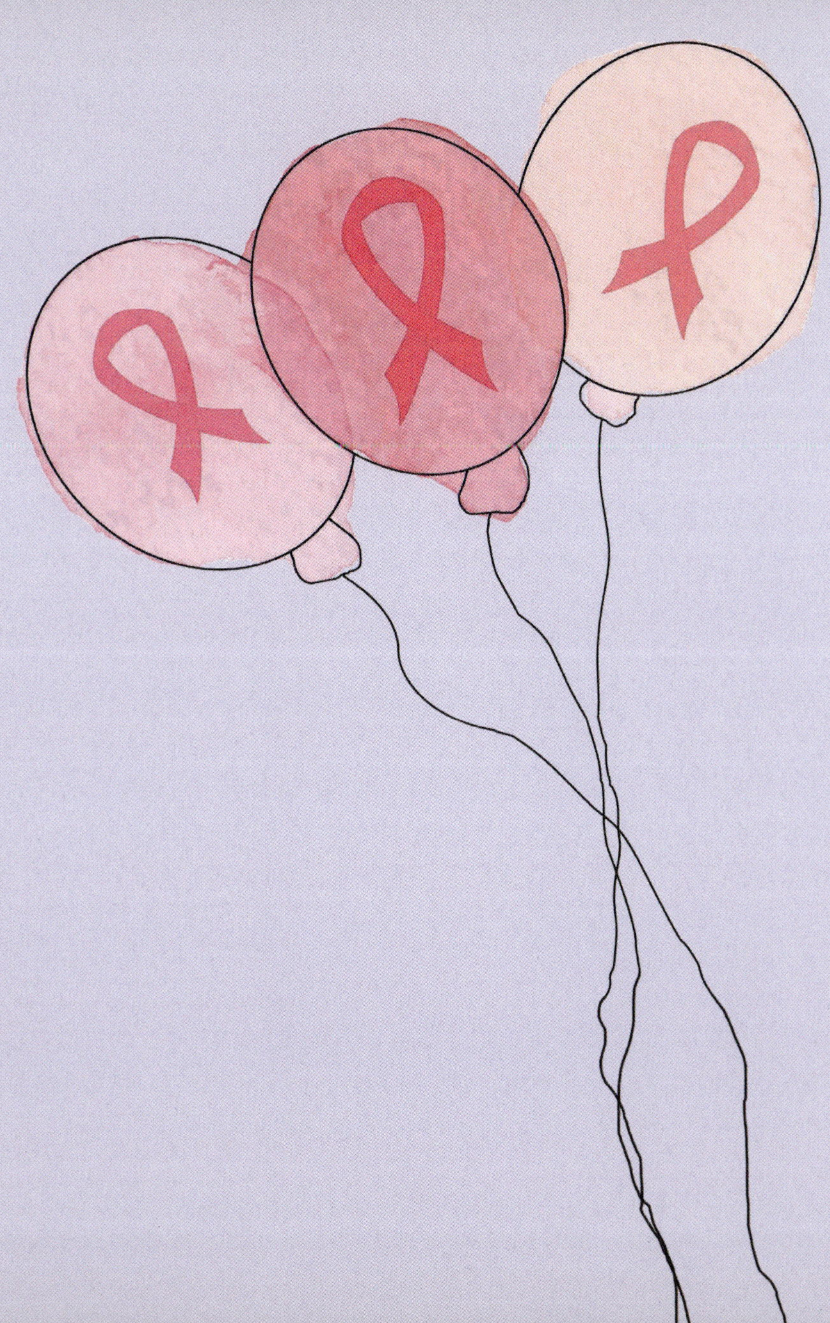

THE HAPPY BOOK was originally born as a personal gift to a friend who was having a double mastectomy for a recurrence of breast cancer. She continues to be an inspiring example of strength and grace to her friends and colleagues, and we all wish her continued good health!

In honor of my friend, and in memory of my beautiful mom who lost her courageous battle with breast cancer in 2005, I am committed to donating a portion of the proceeds from *THE HAPPY BOOK* to organizations working toward a cure.

XXOO

Andrea

Andrea Reiser is a happiness coach, author and writer specializing in positive psychology and gratitude. A contributor to The Huffington Post, Andrea finds joy in Broadway musicals, laughing uncontrollably with lifelong friends and having her feet in the warm beach sand. She is beyond grateful every day for the blessings of her husband and four sons.

Find out more about Andrea at www.andreareiser.com.

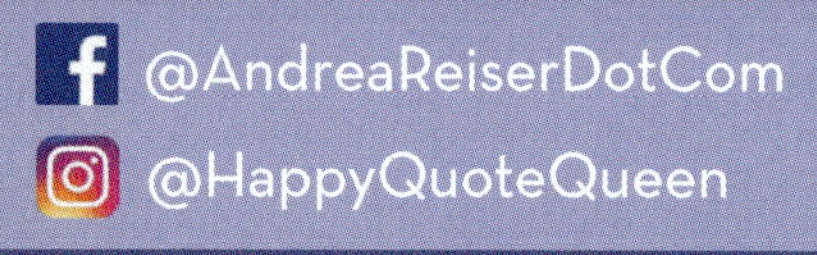